To Mother

May God bless you
to walk in your
divine purpose!

Ms. Linda

2/24/12

MY PURPOSE
Revealed

Ms. Linda, the Nanny—Not Just the Help!

LINDA K. BARNETT

Inspiring Voices®

A Service of **Guideposts**

New International Version Christian Growth Study Bible. Zondervan Corporation, 1997.
Holy Bible, New King James Version. Thomas Nelson Inc., 1979.
Webster's Dictionary.

Inspiring Voices books may be ordered through booksellers or by contacting:

Inspiring Voices
1663 Liberty Drive
Bloomington, IN 47403
www.inspiringvoices.com
1-(866) 697-5313

ISBN: 978-1-4624-0260-1 (sc)
ISBN: 978-1-4624-0259-5 (e)

Library of Congress Control Number: 2012913420

Printed in the United States of America

Inspiring Voices rev. date: 08/28/2012

CONTENTS

DEDICATION AND ACKNOWLEDGMENTS

I dedicate this work to my Family and friends in Ohio and Oklahoma
Also I dedicate this work to the families for whom I worked as a nanny—for each one was a labor borne out of love.

I would like to offer a special thanks to all the people in the body of Christ—my spiritual family—who helped to motivate me to love God more. They are the late Bishop Sherman Taylor and Mother Edna Taylor, Pastor Melvin Cooper and Joyce Cooper, Apostle Layla Caldwell, Elder Johnny Magness and Zandra Magness, Pastor Donald Woody, Pastor Charles Williams, and the late Mother Johnson.

And a special acknowledgment must go to Bishop Gary McIntosh and Pastor Debbie McIntosh and the Greenwood Church Family for motivating and preparing me to walk into the purpose and destiny that God has prepared for me on Earth.

I would be remiss if I failed to acknowledge Kirk Franklin and William McDowell for their inspirational music, which has literally transformed my life, helping me to understand there is purpose in my pain and that the change I wanted to see had to begin first in me. Also I'd like to acknowledge Sarah Young, the author of *Jesus Calling: A 365 Day Journaling Devotional*, whose inspirational book moved me on a daily basis, as it increased my faith and became a tool with which I've blessed so many others.

Last but certainly not least, I send a big shout-out to all my boys in the Pool House Ministry. I reached out my hand but was touched in my heart.

My prayer is that God will bless each and every one of you. May the Lord position you into purpose as your purpose is revealed.

PREFACE

Now as I look back, in the pain there was a plan. Now Lord, I can say, "Thank You" God, for showing me who I am.

Forgiven through his love, and healed by his blood, I am a winner. Life has knocked me down, now I'm standing and I realize that a tear was never wasted. I'm on my way to who I am. I'm stronger through the pain, I've survived!

This last year has been an awesome experience for me. Truly, the presence of God has been evident in my life. I've been changed, set free, and forgiven. In His presence, I have found joy, peace, grace, and favor. Now that I'm in the moment I have waited for, I will not let it pass me by.

I will not go back to the way it used to be.

In this life, I have learned that everyone hurts, everyone goes through sorrow, but if we keep the faith and pray, He heals the hurt. I just got well.

In this life, everyone has his or her own cross to bear. No cross, no crown has brought me to where I am. The weight I had to bear made me strong, and the final price was paid with Christ's amazing grace. I stand in awe of God, ready to go higher.

During this time of elevation, God inspired me to write this book out as part of my journey into my purpose. I thank God for not giving up on me in the process, as He could see in me what I could not. He knew where this journey was carrying me.

I thank God for unexplainable joy, peace that eases my pain, and now he is my everything.   I thank God for cleaning my house, and for cleaning *me*!

LETTERS FROM THE CHILDREN

Letter #1

Linda Barnett has been my nanny for more than half my life. Her influence has done so much for me, and it is because of her I am the person I am today. Linda is a caring, loving, devoted, god-fearing woman of integrity and purpose, and any person who has been blessed enough to know her long enough can vouch for me on that fact. Linda has a way of helping me, and others, in our times of need, not only with the grace and patience of an angel, but also with the humor and liveliness that we need to cheer us up. These are just a few of the qualities that I grew accustomed to at home.

Going off to college this past year, I knew I would miss Linda, but I severely underestimated her impact on my life. I miss being able to see her and discuss my problems. I miss the easy laugh and joyfulness she always brings, but every time I get a text from her, or every time she calls, I am instantly filled with joy and am always sure to laugh.

Linda hasn't just fixed a few problems for me; she has done this for so many. Galatians 4:27 says, "Rejoice, O childless woman, you who have never given birth!

Break into a joyful shout, you who have never been in labor! For the desolate woman now has more children than the woman who lives with her husband!" And with Linda, I know this is true. The impact she has left on me includes a faith in God, a love for others, a respect for elders, and an integrity for all things. This was not just limited to me. My brother, my sister, my cousins, other families, friends, and any people lucky enough to meet her have felt this too. I was just lucky enough to have Linda a lot longer and be around her more than most. God blessed me with the love of Linda Barnett. I can never express how much she has done for me.

D. Boone

Dear. Linda
    Thank you for all you've done. Thank you for the remote control car. I play with it a lot. Also thank you for teaching me to be a good boy and to teach me about God. I hope you like your christmas present.
P.S. You smart, you kind and you important
                                    Love,
                                    Bennett

Letter #2

Linda,

I would just like to start off by saying thank you so much for all you have done for me. I am so glad you have been a part of my life for so long. I know I can always come to you whenever I need something. I love spending good times with you, especially our laughs and girl talks. I would not trade a second we have spent together for anything else.

You mean the world to me. You have taught me so many life lessons, which I really appreciate. I love when you teach me about the stories in the Bible. You try to see the world through my eyes to get my perspective on things so we can really understand the true meaning of things together. My absolute favorite thing is the memories we share and when you call or text to check on me or pray with me.

Lastly, I know you will always be there for me. I can tell you my absolute deepest secrets, and you will not tell a soul. Although sometimes they are bad, you will not look at me in a different way. You help me try to change my ways and pray and use faith to become a better person. Your faith and dedication help me strive to become a better person, and it drives me to become a better Christian.

I love you, Linda, and thank you again for everything. You will always be in my life, and I will never forget a single moment we have shared.

Love you always,
Haley

Chapter 1

JOURNEY TO THE REVELATION
OF MY PURPOSE

My purpose was revealed to me in different visions before I started writing this book. I remember babysitting was my first job as a young girl. As a young lady, I used to babysit two children for my mother's pastor. He was a bank manager, and his wife was a schoolteacher, and they had two boys. Later I started to take care of their house as well, not knowing at the time that this would be my destiny and my purpose. It started with God using a pastor to push me into becoming what God had ordained. It's all about God and the purpose and plan he has for my life.

The first babysitting job was in Ohio. I later moved to Oklahoma. There I joined a church and took care of the pastor's house as well as the church. I landed a job as a nanny with a family-practice doctor and worked with that family for about eleven years.

When I first started working for the doctor's family, they had two girls. They later gave birth to two more children, both boys. They were wonderful children. The girls were three and four years old when I started with them. They were so adorable. I changed their clothes about three times a day because they were such tomboys, and I did not want them to wear dirty clothes. Every time we went out, people just adored them. Later, when the two boys came, they were just as adorable.

I went on to work for a surgeon's family. God blessed me with more great kids, a girl and three boys. I later became their cousin's nanny as well; they also had awesome children.

In this book, I will share my God-given purpose and journey as I recall it. My purpose will most definitely be revealed with experience— it will speak for itself. That is where you will find real wisdom. There is always a message in your experience and a new insight waiting for you in the experiences you've already had. When you find your passion in life, you will know that's what you should do with your life. It will come naturally.

I remember when I first became a nanny. The families did not have to instruct me on every little detail of being a nanny. Not knowing that nannying would be my God-ordained purpose, I just did my best. The families would simply state, "She knows what she is doing."

I remember staying with my grandmother as a little girl. I ran her household whenever I visited her in that small town in Oklahoma called Okmulgee, and I was not even thirteen years old. Later on, as I became an adult and began to pursue a career, I attended travel school in Pittsburgh, Pennsylvania. I did not care for that. After working jobs here and there, I went back to school for early childhood education. Because I knew I liked kids, I thought about being an administrator in an early childhood education center. That never came to pass.

One day, not really knowing what it entailed, I answered an ad in the newspaper for a nanny. The Webster dictionary defines "a nanny as being a child's word for nurse or a trained childcare specialist". I never had children, but I just flowed right into it. That's another sign that helped me recognize my gift and purpose. It came very easily to me. I have been a nanny now for twenty-two years. I never considered that it would become my career when I first began, but it was my purpose—years passed and I never noticed. There's fulfillment and peace when you are walking with purpose in the destiny that God has established for your life on earth.

Establishing positive and productive relationships with parents while being responsible for the care of their most precious jewels—their children—brings structure to their homes. This benefits both children and parents.

In the end, I learned there was purpose in the pain I endured. There were reasons for everything I had to go through to get to the purposeful destiny God had designed for me. We never know what tomorrow will bring. However, one thing I know for sure is that this season made me stronger and more mature.

Abide, abide, abide.

Chapter 2

CHANGE

Whether good or bad, there comes a season of change in every believer's life. Like most who experience these pitfalls in life, I was caught off guard. As Christians, we should always be alert. 1 Peter 5:8-9 tells us to be self-controlled and alert. "Your enemy, the devil, prowls around like a roaring lion looking for someone to devour. Resist him, standing firm in the faith, because you know that your brothers throughout the world are undergoing the same kind of suffering".(NIV)

I had to realize that, just as Christ suffered, so shall we. Just as Christ reigned, so shall we. I'm reminded of a story about Joseph in the Bible. When his brothers were jealous of him and threw him in a pit, he later became governor of the kingdom. One's pit experience will bring one closer to or farther from God, depending on how one choose to go through one's affliction.

"It was good that I was afflicted so that I might learn of your decrees" (Psalms 119:71). Sometimes God's blessing comes through pain and trouble. These are the times you will know His goodness through trusting Him. In other words, it's all good. I thank God for the pit experiences that brought about changes in my life. They took me places I had never been before. They broke off strongholds, struggles, bad habits, and all those little foxes that ruin the vineyards in bloom. I thank God for the grooming that brought a cleansing, reviving, restoring, and renewing in righteousness and faith. I am most grateful for the changes that became purpose.

Sometimes, in order to go up with God, we first have to go down. It's a humbling process that can either reduce or add time. If we, as a people, have ever needed change, I would say it's right now. People are looking for change; they are losing hope. We need His glory. Our hearts need to turn back to God so He can release His miracles, signs, and wonders. Sometimes we don't understand God's time, ways, and methods. He does not always let us see what we shall be; but when we become lost in this thing called life, God allows change to begin.

In order to grow, I had to have some rain, and growing roots included some pain. That was when my faith grew and hot winds blew. It made me stronger. In the fire, I realized I had to die before I could live. In the middle of my pit experience, I had to realize the changes I wanted to see had to first begin in me. Matthew 5:14 says, "You are the light of the world. A city on a hill cannot be hidden." The world is looking for change. My prayer is that if you are looking for Jesus, I hope you find Him in me.

The change I wanted to see began in me. God's plan is perfect when we are not. There is a season for everything, a time to plant, and a time to uproot. God has made everything beautiful in its time.

Purpose revealed.

Change.

Chapter 3

MOVING FROM ONE LEVEL TO ANOTHER

In my journey as a nanny, with each family, God moved me from one level to another. When I first started, I nurtured the children's basic needs. As trust was built, God moved me from one level to the next. I became a trusted friend, counselor, listener, liaison, and a way-maker leading them to the way, the truth, and the light of God.

This greater intimacy changes your position. You become a family member, and that requires honesty and integrity. This honesty and integrity cannot come from what someone hears about you; it comes from what that person sees and knows about you. As I began to communicate more and more deeply with the families I worked with, they began to see me as more than an employee. They began to accept me as part of the family. I laughed when they laughed, cried when they cried, and we all wanted nothing but the best for each other. That's love.

I began to love those children as if they were my own. I worried that they were spoiled. One day, one of the children began to cry because he wanted to go out of town with a friend for the weekend, but he could not go because he had a game. I cried as well. It hurts to see a child cry.

You know, God positioned me as a nanny in those homes and used me in many ways to be helpful to each family. Sometimes we think we only have one gift or certain thing to obtain in life. That means that we limit God in our lives. The Bible says that, with God, all things are possible. Over the years, God used me to help in many different areas with the children and the parents, as well. God is awesome, and I thank Him that I am fearfully and wonderfully made. I learned there is greatness in being in Christ. He is allowing me to see and to walk in His Kingdom.

In my journey, God equipped me with everything I needed to perfect my purpose as a nanny and to become all that He has planned for me. To restore, regain, and retain what God has in store for me, He has put me on assignment. While using me to solve problems and situations, God may be glorified for taking me out of my comfort zone and moving me from one level to the next.

The knowledge I have gained helps me to move forward. As I become aware of biblical truths, I become wiser. I help those who were bitter to become better, all the while realizing what God intended for me—to get my life on the right course. "Many are the plans in a man's heart, but it is the Lord's purpose that prevails" (Proverbs 19:21). This is a scripture I stand on, and it helped as the children grew older.

That is why I have to move. The children do not remain the same, so I have to move with them from one level to another, from one situation to another, with the love and maturity of God. The steps of a good woman are ordered by God. I thank God for my children; He allowed me to affect their lives through Him. They were willing vessels.

Having a strong connection and being committed to a single purpose helps to raise whole, healthy, well-rounded children who are inspired to grow into adults with purpose-driven lives. It's important to have the right connections. Life is a series of relationships that come together to shape our future.

It is so important to be connected to the right people. Right connections enhance the walk into purpose. I was created to interact and connect with the children God put in my path. When you have the right connections, you have something to offer. I began to realize that the right connections and the right relationships help your dreams come alive.

When the divine connects, both parts work and contribute to the same cause. This will leave you feeling fulfilled and edified. You will have disagreements, but you are a family that is committed to working together. So it becomes easy. When you have the same motives, the children will respect you and a friendship will develops. You will not be seen just as the help.

Chapter 4

LIFE AS AN ENCOURAGER

The more God reveals my purpose, the more it becomes like second nature. In other words, pursuing the purpose is just what I do, just like taking a shower every day. Being an encourager is something I love; it inspires people, and it inspires me to inspire people. It also helps me to live a life of confidence and courage.

During this last year of my life, while writing this book, God used me so greatly to inspire and encourage the body of Christ. The office God called me to is that of an Evangelist, which means preacher of the gospel—a revivalist to revive people so that they may live, love, laugh, and dream again. What an honor it is to be chosen by God to bring joy back to someone who has lost it and to be sensitive to others' issues, showing them love and compassion while helping to restore their personal lives.

Being an encourager takes a lot of faith, trust, comfort, wisdom, and most important, sacrifice. It takes a lot of time to listen and show concern for others who lack peace in their lives. I have learned that, in this arena, one must maintain integrity, honesty, and good character in order for people to give their trust to you. In this present state of the world, I thank God for giving me a good foundation and reputation as well as a solid and fruitful life. I attribute my success to living a life of fasting, praying, studying, teaching the Word of God, and applying the Word to my life daily. "So that you may become blameless and pure, children of God, without fault in a crooked and depraved generation in which you shine like stars in the universe—in order that I may boast on the day of Christ that I did not run or labor for nothing" (Philippians 2:15-16).

Encouraging others has been very rewarding for me. Many people confide in me that I came into their lives right on time, just when they were about to give up. This gives me purpose and shows me that my life is as it should be. I would not be able to help someone else if my life were out of order.

I thank God that I have not forgotten some of the things He delivered me from. This keeps me from becoming a self-righteous person. Sometimes people forget where they came from. This is what I love about God. He looks beyond our faults and sees our needs; that's a selah moment. It's so easy to love Him! You will never be able to impart to others what you do not possess yourself. This reminds me of a message that the late Sherman Taylor had preached, "Everybody wants to go to Heaven, but no one wants to die." He did not mean physical death, but to die out of self-righteousness, to sin and live a godly life.

God has used me to evangelize not only by spreading His Word, but also by doing good deeds. I have been led to give money and food or buy new shoes, dresses, purses, books, and daily devotionals. If someone is hungry, he or she doesn't need a prayer; he or she needs some food. Being an encourager requires a lot of sensitivity to the needs of others.

As a nanny, God uses me to encourage the children at all times—through the good times as well as the bad—and that brings about a respect that is valuable to our relationship. The more you teach children how to value people and be respectful, the more meaningful their lives become, and they become a blessing to society. With children, I also learned that if you teach them self-respect and self-worth, they will not struggle with low self-esteem. This is another form of evangelism. See, you have to meet people where they are. "Though I am free from all men, I have made myself a servant to all, that I might win more to Christ" (1 Corinthians 9:19).

Chapter 5

A GOOD NAME

"A good name is more desirable than great riches: to be esteemed is better than silver and gold" (Proverbs 22:1). That comes from righteous living and respect for one another. I did learn, as a nanny, you will wear many hats. You will become just like a family member. It will be very important to have the right connection with children as well as the parents. A nanny is like a second mom.

You know, as the mom, that everyone looks to you for everything. So moms need someone who thinks like they do, who already knows what's on their minds. That is the connection I'm talking about. That will give you a good name, and your family will brag about you to everyone. (That's another way to make a good name for yourself.) It will also open up other doors for you with other families.

But most of all, in order to make a good name, you have to be a person of good character and walk with integrity as well as reliability. Because believe me, you will be tested. You see, most families that have nannies and housekeepers are people with good incomes, so you know there will be money here and there throughout the house—credit cards, checkbooks, jewelry, and all kinds of nice, expensive things.

Now, you know what they say. Some people come into your life as a blessing; others come into your life as a lesson. I'm glad I can say I came as a blessing; I am an honest person who walks in integrity. Those who don't, just won't last in this type of position. But when God gives you a platform to display your purpose and destiny, you will line up with it. That's why I have been able to be a nanny for so long with so many professional families—because of my good name.

In this profession, you will meet a lot of professional people here and there. Believe me, I have learned that they are checking you out.

You will set the tone for how people treat you. Integrity, loyalty, reliability, and faithfulness are all extensions of an excellent spirit. I value my performance on the job, my character, and my moral strength to keep growing and maintaining good morals. Integrity is just what I do as a result of who I am. Honesty is just a state of being true.

Some people come into your life as an asset or liability; I made sure I became an asset. You set your own stage. Having a good name will take you places you've never been before. It's like the difference between having something and being something! I thank God he has me being something and that I have a good name. I would like to leave a legacy of having a good name. I want my name to be R.I.P.E., an acronym for reliability, integrity, professional, and excellence, while establishing positive and productive relationships with families and tailoring to each family's specific need.

I really thank God for my good name in the society we live in today. With all the preposterousness we have in this world today, a good name is a precious jewel. I feel very blessed and grateful to God for being with me and caring enough about me to keep me on the right path of righteous living. He has never given up on me while preparing me to become the person I am today.

My good name, Ms. Linda, will live on in the minds of the children whom God allowed me to care for. As I think about it, it was all orchestrated by God. No matter what God has for you, if you just stick with Him and lean not to your own understanding, he will open your eyes to see everything he has for you. I just thank Him for keeping my name good, all the time, even before I became a nanny. And I intend for my good name to go on and on for generations to come.

Proverbs 13:22 says "a good man leaves an inheritance for his children's children". I pray that the influence that I have had on all the children continues to produce a great harvest of love, peace, joy, kindness, self-control, and gratitude for many years to come, for their children, their friends' children, and their children's children.

Chapter 6

QUALIFICATION

Life is always based on prior life experiences. You will never be able to take anyone where you have not been yourself. In my journey of being qualified, I was birthed out of some right decisions, or I should say righteous decisions. When God puts you in a place or builds a platform for you—no matter what hindering spirits or confusion comes your way—there is nothing man can do to unseat you from that place that God has qualified you to be in. Not that I was this great perfect person, but the spirit of God, which was leading me, was this great person. I had to realize this, and I was powerless to control my own tenacity.

Whatever God brings me through, I know it is to get me to my purpose and destiny and that He will give me the strength to deal with it. Love is God's greatest commandment. God loves children, so He had to qualify me to go into other families' homes and care for them. He gave me the strength to be an example of righteous living as a child of God, to sow seeds in the little ones, and to be a problem solver, a helper, a giver, a healer, and a restorer. He assigned me to loosen and to bind, to declare and decree, to pull down, to pluck up, to change atmospheres and environments, and to say what thus said the Lord.

With God entrusting me to do all that, there was a price to be paid through salvation in Jesus Christ. I had to purge out myself in order to live for God. I had to be tried. I had to go through hardship, pain, rejection, trouble, crisis, and failure. But it was part of the process for my qualification. The struggles built character and fostered wisdom, integrity, trust, faith, wholeness, a sound and right mind, and a spirit to serve and help people. It all gave me enduring power. And most of all, it built love, which was all for my gain because when you are a nanny, you have to serve.

This is what God is calling Christians to do—to serve. God promotes us through serving, so learn how to serve. God put me in this place, and prepared me to serve. Through my service—through His love—I drew families closer to Him. What an honor and a privilege that God would use me in such a manner!

I'm so glad God did not give up on me during my transformation to become what He created me to be. You always have to complete this transforming process before you start doing what it is you are meant to do. Many times we try to do before our process is complete. And that brings failure, and we grow disappointed and become unsuccessful, which brings brokenness. The hardest place to trust God is the place of brokenness and discouragement.

Before you can start again, you have to be healed and restored. Anytime God is qualifying you, it is for adjustment and alignment with divine order in your life. I thank God so much for that divine order because not only am I touching the lives of the children I nanny for now, but also I am reaching the children's children. You see, the children I care for now will remember seeds of God that I have sown in their lives, and they will pass them on. This ministry, this work, makes me a spade for the kingdom of God. With this, He has taken me to places I have never been before.

He has become my God more than He has ever been before. The more God for me and in me is all for Him, glory be.

Chapter 7

RESPECT

This all comes from walking in love, God's greatest commandment. Whatever a man sows, he shall reap. Sow love and respect, and you shall reap love and respect.

One thing about the people I've worked for, they need to know that I care before they will care what I think. They need to know that I am someone who is truthful as well as trustworthy. As a nanny, I am in their homes sometimes more than they are. So I need to respect their homes and values. You see, when you revere someone, you feel comfortable with them in your home and around your children.

Over the years, God opened so many doors for me to serve in His ministry with the children as well as the parents. So each time I ministered in any given situation, it was on purpose and with respect.

Respect brings about reliability, excellence, success, professionalism, empowerment, capability, and trust and forms the acronym, R. E. S. P. E. C. T.

At the same time, this work is about building a loving, respectful family while at the same time being a light for God. Always having an open line of communication to transfer information, helps build a strong relationship. This is how God equipped me to handle my assignment as a nanny. I endeavor always to do my best because I trust in the Lord. The Bible says "it is best to trust in the Lord and acknowledge Him in all our ways, and He will direct our path"-Proverbs 3:5(NIV). I believe whatever God starts, He will orchestrate. Where God guides, he provides.

In my position as a nanny, I learned that people who respect you also honor you and give you credit for honesty. This brings a good reputation. What a way to represent God, especially in the time we live in now! God says, "Those who honor me, I will honor." I thank God for trusting and honoring me to be a part of so many great families and to let my life be my witness.

I believe that where your treasures are, that's also where your heart is. I try to make sure my treasures are the right stuff—love, kindness, peace, joy, and respect. When a mother respects you, it helps her to trust you as a nanny in her home. It brings about comfort to the children as well. And when it's your God-given purpose, you just flow with it.

Chapter 8

EXCELLENCE

Excellence is a great merit. Being a person of excellence, you value yourself and your performance in all that you do. If you do not value yourself, how can anyone value you? I once heard someone say that people treat you according to how you treat yourself. Your character is your moral strength, and its integrity—what you do as a result of who you are—will keep you in a state of truth. Faithfulness will help you remain loyal and reliable, which along with the following list, are the attributes of excellence.

- Value
- Character
- Integrity
- Honesty
- Faithfulness

And when you achieve these attributes, they must be used as your tools of power. As I was becoming what God had ordained for me to become, I realized it would take preparation and strength because I was marked by the majesty of God to fulfill destiny and purpose. Having moral strength and moral standards to uphold was beneficial to the children, who exemplified excellence. Now, if you are out of order, they will let you know. All through the years, while being under the authority of a great God, I strived for excellence in all things—my word, my integrity, my works, my efforts, and my commitment to my families.

15

After working with my first family, I did not have to look for others; they sought me out. That came from having an excellence spirit; people come to me. "But to the saints that are in the earth and to the excellent, in whom is all my delight" (Psalms 16:3). Whatever we are doing, we are doing it unto God, which changes lives as we serve in excellence. My character, my word, my self-worth, my faithfulness, and my loyalty to my families kept me going as a nanny for the past twenty-two years.

I will always strive to work in excellence in order to help raise responsible, loving, caring, children and so that they will be prepared for the many paths of life, which sometimes take abrupt turns. But through much prayer and teaching, they will be equipped for the journey and not get weary. "With your help, I can advance against a troop with my god I can scale a wall" (Psalms 18:29).

God's a God of excellence without limitations or boundaries.

Chapter 9

COMPASSION

Being a nanny, I have learned that I am very compassionate. I always knew that I was, but becoming a nanny really revealed it. When working with children, compassion is a must-have. Nannies and compassion go together. I look up *nanny* in my dictionary; the definition was "a child's word for nurse that takes compassion."

I think that I am compassionate because God has shown so much compassion toward me. I once had someone pray to me, and they said that God had wrapped me in love, layer by layer. So I guess if I'm full of so much love, compassion will just flow out. That's why God positioned me in the career that I have; it's family oriented, and family is all about love and compassion toward one another. That's why you have to show people you care before they care to hear what you think or say.

I also believe that's why it is so important to live a life of compassion; it just stirs something up in others. It shows that you care. The most successful times with the children I cared for were when I corrected them with compassion. It built trust, which, in turn, nurtured relationships. This has helped me to be successful with the children as well as the parents, who could see the relationships growing. Sometime the children told me things that they were dealing with before they told their parents because they knew I would show compassion and help with the situation.

I was so honored when God moved one of my oldest boys to start a Bible discussion group with teenage boys. They enjoyed our groups. They actually showed up, were honest, asked me to pray about the issues they faced, and dealt with things openly. So what they learned in our group meetings spilled over into their friendships as well. As the word got around, other teens wanted to attend or start their own groups at home. I believe God wants us all to be change agents and do something different.

When you are walking in destiny and purpose, it spills over into everything else. Your own uniqueness helps you to know who you are. "All things work together for good to them that love God, to them who are called according to His purpose" (Romans 8:28). What God has done in me, by my living a life of inspiration and compassion, can be expressed outwardly. The seeds that I have sown into their lives will remain forever, not only for them, but for their children's children. This takes me back to why we are here, and it is to serve people, that's how we get to greatness, serve your way to it, so we will be able to give all the glory to God.

I met so many lovely families and worked in lovely homes in my nanny career, I know God qualified me to become a nanny before I ever started working as one. It was like being trained on the job, but I was trained by God. You see, my training was going to be used for sowing the seeds of the kingdom of God. While things were being established, restored, regained, and refreshed in their lives, I realize how much compassion God had for me on Calvary.

Chapter 10

LOYALTY

In this world, I strongly believe that if you ever plan on making a difference, you will have to show loyalty, which is faithfulness. As a nanny and Christian, I have learned that the loyalty of others is something you earn by your actions and the way you treat people. God helped me to show loyalty toward my families. God has been so faithful to me, and whatever we do, we should do it as we would unto Christ. So being loyal just comes naturally to me. When you are faithful, it opens many other doors because you are a person people can count on, depend on, and trust. It just adds to your good name.

I thank God that he has chosen me to be a loyal, faithful person. What an honor it is, and I give all the glory to God. Loyalty is surely a state of being. It took a lot of loyalty as well as faithfulness unto myself to complete this book. I realize I could never process what I did not pursue. This took loyalty, faithfulness, and focus. As a nanny, I had a whole family depending on me to be all of these at once.

Trust is brought about when you are loyal and respect the values and standards of a family's household. I feel my loyalty perfects my honesty. But I had to do what I did as unto God, and He blessed my life through each family. You can't help but be blessed when you are chosen by God. You will have the credibility as well as the reliability. Credibility determined my reliability, and my reliability determined my credibility. It was trust. And that came about as God made me whole and healthy. Out of that, he produced integrity, excellence, reliability, and professionalism in me.

While taking a licking, I keep on ticking. It helps me to bond with children as well as the parents. They become family to me—to listen, comfort, and support—in every aspect of life, through good times and bad,. Being a nanny is a huge responsibility; you must always be at the top of your game because you are caring for children, our most valuable, most precious jewels.

I have learned to value the three things that a nanny defines: loyalty, commitment, and honesty. These were very crucial and paid off for me in a lifetime of influence. They enabled me to have a good reputation in my community, in my church, and as an evangelist for Christ. In this regard, I was held to the highest standards, both publically and privately, which has helped me and other nannies to stay loyal. "Provide things honest in the sight of all men" (Romans 12:17(AKJ).

Chapter 11

GOD POSITIONED ME FOR GREATNESS

"God did this so that, by two unchangeable things in which it is impossible for God to lie, we who have fled to take hold of the hope offered to us may be greatly encouraged. We have this hope as an anchor for the soul, firm and secure" (Hebrews 6:18-19).

God positioned me in my personal life as well as my career to be His constant companion. While experiencing His presence and His peace, He used me to encourage others while enjoying my journey. God showed me that all the trials and tribulations that I endure were not even about me. Rather, they were all a teaching, training, and elevation exercise to elevate my relationship to Him, and it was all for my good. He let me know that, as long as I stay with Him, I will enjoy His presence on the journey. He also let me know there's a price to be paid for greatness in Him; through all of life's up and downs, I have to keep the faith that He sees the invisible, believes the incredible, and receives the impossible.

Even though I trust and believe God, I have often wondered why I have had to go through certain things, but as I walk them out I realize it was all for my experience and growth. I used to think, *Well, God, just do what You do. Why do you have to take me through so much change—like a metamorphosis? God, please just make everything right.* But then I ask myself, *What would I learn from that? I had to go through tests and trials. No test, no testimony, right?* All is used to help others while being in a position of greatness.

It took some struggles. It was kind of like the story of Joseph as he was put in the pit in the Bible., It's like a dark place in your life, but you just have to know how to work your affliction while in the pit, or in the darkness, in your life. God dealt with me deeply, some for good and some for not but in the end, it was all good. In other words, right before you live, you have to die.

Die out of pride, selfishness, and self-control. It's the little foxes that spoil the vine (Song of Solomon 2:15). And it's like this right before you live; you have to die out to self, to live out your dreams and all that God has for you. And a lot of times, not dying out will hold you hostage or in bondage from your past. I had to learn to let go of my past so I would not forfeit my future, my purpose, and my God-given destiny. Through intimacy in my relationship with God, He transformed me from the inside out, into the one He desired me to be. For we are not our own, to Him (God) we belong, so I learned how to give myself away to others so that God may be glorified. "And we all, who with unveiled faces, reflect the Lord's glory, are being transformed into His likeness with ever-increasing glory, which comes from the Lord, who is the Spirit" (2 Corinthians 3:18).

Chapter 12

LET ME COME TO A CITY NEAR YOU

This chapter was borne out of one of my kids after we had a prayer to thank God for her turning twenty-one, becoming an adult, and making some decisions. A light was turned on to choices that bring knowledge. Darkness will keep people ignorant and will cause chaos and confusion in their lives. Everything will be present but out of order, and I refuse to let any of my children be lost in darkness. They will be law-abiding citizens.

God allowed me to see a lot as a nanny—mainly how the better half-lives. All of the people I worked for were doctors. It helped me to value life and what is really valuable in life and to be grateful. I also realized things and money do not make you whole. Because we all know that, in this life, we shall have trials and tribulations. Thinking peace comes from having enough money, possessions, and alarm systems are backward. So is trying to deny the inevitable effects of aging. And none of these things surpass the peace of God.

One weekend, I had to stay over with the kids. A year before that, I had started a Bible study group with about six friends of one of the young men whom I had been a nanny for. One day, one of the young men had come over, and he said, "Linda, I need you to pray for me to get the devil off my back. I know God put you in my life to help me."

When you are on assignment from God, he assigns you to everybody in the circle, and he will definitely enlarge your territory. When the young man asked for my help, I became obligated to help him. That's my job as a servant of God; it's my purpose as well as my destiny. When God calls you to service, your life, destiny, and purpose are His. Gender, color, religion— none of those matter. You just have to be open to be used by God.

I love the position God call me to. When you love it, that's a sign that your purpose. If you don't feel like it's a job, it's just what you do. I realized that the more I became like God; the more he developed me into the unique person He designed me to be. It reminds me of the scripture in 1 John 3:2, "Let your light shine before men so God may be glorified." On Sunday evenings, I usually take time out to call some of my kids who are in college to encourage them to stay focused, even with all their newfound freedom, and to pray and instill in them that they are leaders. You can't do that and make them listen to you if you are not living that example and being their role model and letting the light of God shine through you.

Bishop Taylor would always say, "One thing about young people is that they will call you out on your character." These kids do not realize how much they impact my life as I walk upright before God and man. They really help me to keep a straight and narrow path. When God puts you in your purpose, it all works for your good. I was explaining to one of my kids, who are in college, that in life, you will always be tested. Until you pass each test, you will keep coming back to it, just like in school. You do not go from one grade to the next without passing a test. It's the same in life; there will be tests we have to conquer before we can move ahead.

"Beloved now we are children of God; and it has not yet been revealed what we shall be, but we know that when he is revealed, we shall be like Him, for we shall see Him as He is" (1 John 3:2). I am grateful that God was able to trust me with such great opportunities to impact young people's lives.

One thing I have learned, is that there are lessons of trust sent by God which are sometimes wrapped in difficulties. But the benefits far outweigh the costs. Well-developed trust will bring you many blessings, not the least of which is the peace of God, which He has promised to keep us in perfect peace. Though you lose everything else, if you gain the peace of God, you will be rich indeed.

Chapter 13

ON MY WAY TO WHO I AM

We all talk about purpose and destiny. Once you find out your purpose, the reason you are here on earth, that's when you start to live. Purpose is not about money or a job—that is what you do, so it's just your nature. You live to pursue, and then you do. We all have a process in life that we have to go through. Crisis, trouble, rejection—these do not discriminate. They show up in everyone's lives. They are just a part of life that help and teach us to trust. If you never had a reason to have faith in God, you would never know Him.

Being a Christian is a walk of faith, and it is difficult to worship a God you cannot see. Life has knocked all of us to our knees a few times, but there has never been a tear wasted, for those tears strengthened us to become who we are. They have helped me to become who I am and to walk in destiny and purpose, so I can be what God has called me to be and receive every blessing God has for me. To leave a legacy that I, Linda K. Barnett, was once here. Without His blessing, I would have never known that life is much more than *things*. Life is how you live, and you must be able to answer the question, *what did your life really mean?* It's like you have to die of fear, so you can live. Right before I lived, I had to die.

The scripture says "He came to give us life and life more abundantly" John 10:10(NIV).

God came to give life. Right now, I feel like I can touch the sky. I enjoyed being a nanny so much because I became a problem solver, a server, and that's why God put us here, to serve and to help with problems. It says a lot when people can trust you with the lives of their family members, God with His people! What an honor and a privilege that God would trust me with such a huge task. Every time I think about it, I stand in awe of Him. He put such great families in my life. The children (wow) have a great personal relationship with me, I love them so, and they love me as well. What a connection! And I can truly say that we are family. Anyone who has ever seen me interact with my families will testify that it never was about race. It was about love for one another, and that's what love is. We are there for each other through the good, the bad, and the ugly. But it's all good; God is allowing me into the children's lives as a nanny and a trusted friend.

Chapter 14

LARGE AND IN CHARGE (LO-LO)

They say big things come in small packages.

As I began my journey as a nanny, I knew I would have new births, but I never thought I would deal with death. And yet death is a part of life; that's why it's so important to live your life well, to be an inspiration to others and treat people well. LoLo was my first. She and her sister were adorable little blonde girls with great big hearts. LoLo was the oldest, but she was tiny in stature. However, once she opened her mouth, you knew she was the oldest, wisest one.

I remember one time we were at the YWCA, and some other, bigger girls were there swimming, and they were bothering her little sister. LoLo got in the pool where they were, and she grabbed the girl by her swimsuit and said, "That's my little sister; leave her alone."

I was sitting there thinking, *oh my goodness!* Well, they did not have any more problems with those girls after that.

LoLo was definitely a leader. She loved life. She was born with heart problems, but she never let them hold her back. She accomplished anything she put her mind to. She helped me look at life in a whole different light, and that's probably the reason I can write this book.

I think about the song Tim McGraw sings, called "Live Like You Were Dying," when I think about how she lived.

She inspired me and so many others to believe that there are no limitations in life and to be grateful for life. I always had to take a second look at her and be careful about some of my conversations with her. I had to remember that she was a child and not an adult, even though she was wise beyond her years. She loved her little sister and always watched out for her. You could not be around her and have a bad day; she would say or do something to inspire you, and I know it's because of her that I'm a better person. She was always large and in charge, and I thank God for giving me an opportunity to be a part of her wonderful life. I feel blessed to have been a part of her upbringing.

LoLo passed away. Her heart worked as hard as it could. She gave out so much love, but I believe God did allow her to fulfill her life's destiny and purpose on earth, and then He called her home to dance with the angels. She became a confident, strong, and faithful young woman.

Before LoLo passed, her parents gave birth to two wonderful little boys. They were the best children I ever nannied. Well, I feel that way about all the children I've worked with!.

One day, when I had decided to write a book about my experience and purpose as a nanny, I ran across a letter Loren had written me when I no longer was her nanny. We remained family, and the letter says it all. It left me speechless with tears streaming down my face; she was so awesome and always large and in charge. With the permission of her mother, I have included a copy of LoLo's letter in this book.

Rest in peace, Lo-Lo.

up down Allaround
Hey waz ↑,↓,ⓔ,

        I miss you so much!
mabey we can do something
togeather sometime! Like go
to the mall or just go
to the park! You were a great
friend and I am always
here for you! How is it going?
I'm ok but my grades arn't
so swell! I miss having you
around and I hope we can
keep in touch!
                        Love
                        LoLo

P.s. write back
whenever you can I would love
to ▓▓▓▓ ▓▓▓▓ whats up with you.
And just to let you know I
always here is you need!

P.s I love you & what you
have taught me! Thanks to
you I am now bealiving in
▓▓ God & ▓▓▓▓ Jesus!
        catch ya later & let God be with
                bye!! you! →

Oh ▓▓▓▓ won't did I
tell you that I am
going out with Dustan
don't tell any body ▓▓▓
because he does not want
any body to Know!

                    bye,
And again, Let God be
with you!

Chapter 15

BOYS IN THE POOL HOUSE

Wow! Every time I think about this pool-house ministry, all I can think is, *wow! Look at God.* While mentoring one of the young men that I was a nanny to, his friends often came over to hang out. And being who I am, I would always act as witness about God to them. God allows me to be in contact with many people in many different facets of life, and I think of myself as their "gospel mail carrier." As God allowed me to encourage and speak to their lives, they began to tell their friends about what I said. This is how the pool-house ministry came into being. As more of their friends started showing up, we began meeting in the pool house at the home where I was working.

During the last couple of years, on Sunday evenings, we got together and had a little fellowship to discuss the Bible and their issues, and we used the Word of God to work it out. Sometimes they said things that made my hair stand on end, but I thank God for their honesty. I Corinthians 9:19 says, "Though I am free and belong to no man, I make myself a slave to everyone, to win as many as possible to Christ." I thank God for their honesty and reality, as so many adults walk around with masks on, saying one thing but living another. That's why there's no change. True deliverance and change comes from honesty and dealing with your issues. Just like a person sweeping a floor—instead of picking the dirt up and throwing it in a trash, if they sweep it under the rug, it does no good.

I count it an honor and a privilege that God allowed me to speak into the lives of these boys. Not only that, but also that their parents would have that trust and respect for my character to allow me to minister to their children is an honor. Matthew 5:16 says, "Let your light shine before men that they may see your good deed and praise your father in heaven." God gets all the glory. I praise Him for equipping me to reach a young generation of leaders. These young men do not come from broken homes; they all come from good homes with successful parents who are well off.

See, you can want more of God; that's not uncommon. When your life is all messed up, you are broke, busted, and disgusted. But these young men had material things that some adults would never acquire. I believe God is going to bless them for taking the time, at their young ages, to learn of Him. It will be with them all of their lives; they will remember the pool-house ministry with Ms. Linda whenever they face difficult situations in life. In God's eyes and His word, it is not always what you see, but rather, it's how you see it.

I love those young men as if they were my sons. I pray for them continuously. Some weekends, I text them to encourage them to make right choices and to let them know I'm here for them. As they become adults, this will always stick with them. They will be able to share their experiences with their own children about Ms. Linda, their friend's Afro-American nanny. I have to add that these boys never looked at me as being of a different race, nor did I see them that way, either. It was all good, and I always let them know they were courageous, strong, mighty men of God!

LETTERS FROM THE BOYS OF
THE POOL HOUSE MINISTRIES

Letter #1

Linda,

Thank you for everything you do for me. You have been in my life for as long as I can remember and have always been there for me to give me guidance and strength in myself and in the Lord. When we are doing Bible study, I feel it's a release from the troubles I might be going through in my life, and I can relax and listen to your advice as well as explain my beliefs and feelings. You make the class fun and exciting every day with your jokes and laughter. All of us are very thankful for what you do for us, and I find it difficult to believe that I am going off to college and won't be able to laugh and talk with you every day. You have been one of the biggest influences in my life, and I am very glad that I can call you my friend.

Love,
Baylor

Letter #2

Dear Linda,

I have only known you for a short amount of time, but you have really impacted my spiritual life. Your passion for Christ is so inspiring. I've been to Catholic schools my whole life, but you make it easier and fun to learn about God. You are a great role model to all of us. I have a lot of respect for you, and I wish I could have known you for longer. I sincerely enjoy listening to you talk about God.

Sincerely,
Rocco

Letter #3

Ms. Linda,

What you do for us is one of the highest callings in life. You don't have to teach us more about God and the Bible on your Sunday afternoons. You give up your time every Sunday just to help us high school guys become better people and closer to God.

The best thing about you is you don't just come in and lecture us about how we might be bad people, but you come in and try to help us with the problems we might have and pray with us to help solve the problems. We can tell you anything in the world, and you won't judge us and think that we are bad people. You help us instead of make fun of us. You are a shoulder to lean on with our deepest, darkest secrets. In hard times, you always seem to pop up and give me a call and pray with me. This means the world to me. I can honestly say I love you and thank you for everything you have done and will do for me. You're the best.

Love,
Erik

Letter #4

Linda,

If someone asked me who the best role model or influence in my life was, I would tell them this: "My Bible-study teacher, Linda. She always has the best intentions for us in mind. No matter what, I know that she is a person I can call upon to receive advice or help in any situation. She really does want to bring us closer to God. I believe Linda is a woman God put in my life to strengthen my faith in the Lord. I not only believe this for me, but also for the rest of the guys in our Sunday-night group. Linda truly cares about us and our relationship with the Lord, and for that I am very grateful. She is such a strong person and a great influence on me and the rest of the guys."

Cale

Letter #5

Ms. Linda,

Throughout my years of high school, Ms. Linda has taught me how to become a better Christian and how to deal with things in life through prayer and understanding. She is one of the best people I know and is a great role model. She understands everything that young people are going through and can help us get through it. Ms. Linda has taken the time out of her busy life to spend time with our Bible study group. She can relate to some of the situations we are in and work them out with us. She is a very unselfish person, and we are very blessed to have spent time with her.

Every Sunday that we have Bible study, we read out the Bible, and she teaches us the meaning of all the stories. We are not always well behaved, but she deals with us anyway with a great sense of humor. That being said, we all have love and respect for Ms. Linda and everything she does for us. At the end of each study, she asks us if we need anything in our life to be prayed for, and she will pray for us. She focuses on us and how she can help, and she never asks for anything in return. She is very kind and generous, and she encourages us to be the best that we can be. Her goal is to bring us all closer to God. I am very lucky to have someone so influential, like Ms. Linda, in my life.

Phillip

Chapter 16

HOW TO BE THE BEST NANNY AND HOW TO FIND THE BEST NANNY

Years ago, I started giving the mother of the children I cared for a devotional calendar, and we had a prayer to set off each new year. Whether we are ready or not, each year will bring about some good times, victories, and successes, as well as bad times, failures, and crises. I think preparation is a vital key in life, as we are striving to trust and have faith in God. I always say, I want people in my life who will be assets. Life can sometimes cause you to feel like you are in a terrible pit. That's why I don't want anyone who will throw dirt on me while I'm in the pit; I want people who will help me get out. That's why a nanny must take the long view and think about destiny and know everyone has purpose in life. There will be times when someone or something happens to make life feel like its worthless.

I will not say being a nanny is an easy job; on the contrary, it's a job that comes with a lot of responsibility. You will be dealing with a family's most beloved treasure, their children, as well as their home and precious valuables.

How to Be the Best Nanny

Being a nanny is nothing you can take lightly, and believe me, there will be challenges whenever there are two women in the house. But when it's your purpose, all things work together for those who love God and are called according to His purpose. I have worked for three mothers in my lifetime as a nanny and had great relationships with all three. They were like my sisters from another mother; all three have a special place in my heart. We got along very well. As a nanny, you will have to be dedicated to providing reliability, integrity, professionalism, and excellence (R.I.P.E) while establishing positive and productive relationships with families.

A nanny usually takes on many roles:

Childcare provider
Housekeeper
Counselor
Personal assistant
Cook
Neighborhood babysitter
School homework helper
Errand runner
House sitter
Pet sitter

It will take real dedication. Being a nanny in the Tulsa, Oklahoma area for the past twenty-two years, I've learned that families are looking for someone who can provide them with quality peace of mind. I really enjoy being a nanny because I love children, and they love me. You have to establish a relationship built on trust and respect for each other.

You also need to be a take-charge person. I learned quickly that the parents didn't have time to sit and tell me every little thing that needed to be taken care of. I found also that it never hurts to go beyond the call of duty. You have to have the mind-set that it's not about *money* because the parents are doctors, lawyers, or Indian chiefs. If you do right by them, they will do right by you. I have been so blessed with gifts, money, and support from every family I have worked with. It's all about supporting each other.

Have moral strength and high moral standards because this will be beneficial to the children and will produce excellence in them. Character says a lot about people, and your character will be reflected in the children. In fact, your character can play a part in your salary; it's your self-worth. Your reputation is representative of your character, your very nature. That's why it's so important to leave jobs in good standing, always striving for excellence.

Your reputation will represent your character. The following are some tips for having good character:

Be a good communicator. Always let your employer know about changes and things in your life that will affect your job with them.

Do not waver. Commit to what you say you will do. Do not sway or hesitate in times of concern.

Be a person of your word. Bishop Sherman Taylor, told me a story once about his brother. He said that if he went to a store or some business wanting to purchase something, but did not have the funds to do so, he would just have to say, "Put it on my brother Fred Taylor's account," and he could get it. This was all because he had a good name for keeping his word. This built trust and character. In other words, say what you mean, and mean what you say. It's called commitment to your family. It was not just a commitment for me; my job was about changing lives.

How to Find the Best Nanny

"In all your ways acknowledge Him, and He shall direct your paths" (Proverbs 3:6).

Finding a person with a good character and high moral standards is very important. This is why, in the day and time we're living in, you have to check a person out to see what he or she is about. You want to know about his or her reputation because that will represent his or her character. And that will only come in communication, in honoring the person's word, without wavering. Say what you mean, and mean what you say.

Look for a person who seems to value him or herself. A person's self-worth is very important. If she values herself, she will value your family. You know, the Bible advises "make your request known unto me" (Philippians 4:6). Pray for someone truthful and trustworthy. After all, your children are your most valuable treasure. Honesty will play a great role; it's the state of being truthful with no hidden agenda. You do not have room for error when it comes to your children. When you hire a nanny, you are opening your family up to him or her.

Ask God to purify your heart to see. We have to always remember that man looks at the outer appearance, but God looks at your heart (1 Samuel 16:7). This is why it's so important to acknowledge God in prayer. That's something you can't put a price on or pay for.

Check out credentials, experience, and special training. Communication will be essential for you and your children in this transition.

Being a good nanny leads to letters of recommendation: Make sure to ask for these. They will speak to the nanny's experience and her strengths. Here is a sample:

July 26, 2006
To Whom It May Concern:

It is an honor to introduce Miss Linda Barnett to you.

I have known Linda for sixteen years. My son and her "charges" at the time were childhood friends. I was a stay-at-home mom then, and our little group spent many happy days together. Linda became a close friend of mine, and I can speak highly of her integrity, wisdom, heart, and humor.

I believe Linda has a gift for relating to children. One quality I have admired in her is her ability to recognize the unique strengths of a young person's personality and accentuate it. Children sense that and respond accordingly. It is a talent for lifting their self-esteem without patronizing them. She was a calming presence, yet she has well defined boundaries, which also gives children a sense of security. She is a good communicator, expressing herself honestly and clearly with adults and children alike. Her contagious laugh and sense of humor have carried her a long way in life.

If you are reading this letter of recommendation, you are probably considering her and her team for a nanny service. Because of the qualities I have referred to and what I have witnessed in her life, she has good instincts about others, and seems to draw fine people to her. Any family would be fortunate to have Miss Linda Barnett involved in the care of their most precious gifts, their children. She truly is "good as gold."

Sincerely,
Gloria T., RN

Chapter 17

COMMUNICATION

Communication will be your number one working tool with your families. It will help so much in the long run, and it stops a lot of confusion. I'm a firm believer in setting the record straight. It will work out well for you and the family if everyone keeps the lines of communication open at all times. Let the family know about any credentials, experience, or training you have, as this is very important. As with any job, it will affect your salary and benefit.

As a nanny it is also very important that you offer important information about the child to the parents. As the child is transitioning into having a nanny, discuss in advance who will set and enforce limits. Also, determine the mode in which information will be transmitted. How will you exchange thoughts or give messages, etc. Some people love to receive e-mails at work with updates about their children, and others do not. Discuss this in advance.

The following will be important to communicate to the parents:

The child is not sleeping or eating well.
The child is taking prescribed or non-prescribed medications.
The child is demonstrating behavioral problems. (Be careful about discussing problems and concerns in front of the child.)

The following will be important for the health of your relationship with the children:

Be supportive of each other while going through transition.

Respect the children's feelings by making them feel special, important, and loved.

Always communicate with the children during this transition in their lives.

Means of Communicating

I remember, as a young girl, we moved from Kansas to Ohio. My mother let us know we were moving, but she didn't prepare us for the transition of the move. Not only were we transitioning to a new school, but also to a new city, new neighborhood, and new friends. We had no friends, and the only family we had there was our grandfather. There were also some close friends of my mom's who raised her when her own mom died.

For me, this transition to a new city was very scary because I had never been to Ohio before. Had we visited the city prior to actually moving there, I believe that it may have not been so frightening. So I can relate to the fear of bringing a new person into the home; this can be a very scary transition for a child. This is why I suggest starting off slowly. It's good to start by having the nanny come into the home a couple of hours a day with a parent also being present if possible. It's also good for the nanny to end the day with a "good bye" or "see you tomorrow," each day rather than just slipping away. That way, the child will know the nanny is only going away temporarily.

Chapter 18

FAITHFULNESS AND LOYALTY

The two things you will need if you want to be a successful nanny—faithfulness and loyalty. They are a must. You must possess these two characteristics because they go together like a hand and glove. This brings trust which will create loyalty and faithfulness.

You have to realize that, when you become a nanny to a family, they have open themselves up to you. They are counting on you to help bring structure, stability, and equilibrium to their family. So if you don't have balance and stability in your life, you can't bring it into someone else's life, and you surely can't supply them with faithfulness and loyalty. It must come from within your heart and be what you are made of. You have to have substance. When you are blessed with a family and serving in a faithful and loyal manner, you will become an asset and not a liability to that family.

Being a faithful and loyal nanny who can be trusted has earned me many rewards and unexpected blessings from the families I have served. I've come to realize that loyalty and faithfulness earns not just gifts, but also the respect of the people I worked for. When you are faithful and loyal, you receive the same in return. It's called the law of reciprocation. The Bible puts it simply; "do unto others as you would have them do unto you" Matthew 7:12(NIV).

Over the years, my time there in the household has helped me build a closer bond with each family member. Being loyal has built trust as well with each of them. It's nothing you can buy; you have to show it. Like I said before—become it and possess it.

"Most men will proclaim each his own goodness; But who can find a faithful man?" (Proverbs 20:6).

Chapter 19

RELIABILITY AND AVAILABILITY

Reliability, meaning to depend on and to trust confidently, is hugely important. As a nanny, you will see and hear things that will have to be kept confidential. Most of the time, you are in the house with the children more than the parents are. They will need your trust as well as your discretion. Have you ever heard the saying, "Your word is your bond"? This means that others trust what you say and are able to rely on you, knowing you will be reliable as well as available to their family when needed.

This not just a nine-to-five job; at times, it's more of a twenty-four-hour job, depending on the family. So reliability and availability will play a very big part in being a nanny. If you are a person with a lot going on in your own personal life or family, you really have to know if you can juggle the two. If not, this may not be the profession for you. Most professionals have busy lives and are looking for someone who can be available at the drop of a hat.

Availability means you are accessible for use at all times and contact with you is easily made. Remember, when you are available, sometimes you will not be going home on time. You have to know that fits your lifestyle.

Chapter 20

MORALS AND VALUES

For the purposes of this book, morals are rules or habits conducted by an individual, and values refer more to monetary or material worth. A person's worth is very valuable; it's a part of his or her self-worth and self-esteem. However, you should always value yourself as a person, whatever your occupation.

As people, we all have our own morals, values, and beliefs for our lives and our families. However, it is very important for a nanny to know and come around to the fact that, although the family may make you feel like you are part of their family, this in reality is not your family. As a nanny, you are not there to enforce your morals and values on their family; rather, you are there to respect and abide by the family rules in their households. You have to be able to separate the two, or you will not work out for all families.

In time, as relationships and trust are formed, you both will come to respect each other's values. In the event that their values and morals should interfere with your job as a nanny, you may need to re-examine your employment with this particular family should unresolvable conflict arise. This is why it is so important to communicate early in the employment. That way you can find families that may share similar values and morals. In other words, just make sure it's a good fit! Then you can become an asset to the family God has blessed you with to help nurture, love, and respect. Remember you are not there to change their morals or values unless it's welcomed in a positive way to help change some negative behaviors.

Be faithful and diligent, and become a witness with your life, sharing and giving what God has invested in you. As a nanny, you should value your family, the bonds that will be formed, and the amount of influence you will have on the children and the parents.

Chapter 21

HONESTY

As a nanny, you are not just an employee, but a trusted friend. You are someone they will confide in at all times, sometimes more so than their relatives or closest friends. Honesty will play a huge role. You will not only be with their children, but also you will be trusted with their most valuable assets, their homes, their family businesses, and their family issues. As a nanny, you need to be an honest person, which means being able to be truthful, to have self-control, and to make the right decisions. You will face temptation when working in these professionals' homes, as they leave valuables such as cash, jewelry, and credit cards around the home. These things can be tempting, but you've got to be honest and trustworthy. We are living in times where there is not that much honesty, integrity, or trustworthiness. I'm reminded of an incident in Iraq involving an American soldier turning on American troops. There's nothing worse than an inside job, when it's not just anybody who betrayed you, but it was someone you trusted in your own home.

The late Bishop Sherman Taylor would always say, "I can respect a crook more than a lying hypocrite. At least the crook is being honest about who he is." You have to examine yourself and who you are. "To thine own self be true!" (Shakespeare)

To all the great nannies to be, I'm going to let you in on a great secret. There will be times when you will be tempted. You may be broke, busted, and disgusted at some point, and temptation and wrong thinking will come your way. But wrong will never be right; honesty and righteousness will always outweigh wrong. If the family can and does trust you, trust them also, and they will bless you. You will not even have to ask; they will just give. Honesty will pay off.

Remember the old saying, "Honesty is the best policy."

"There's a blessing in *trust*." Being a great nanny comes with many great rewards.

Honesty will grow your reputation and will bless your life. Honesty will open doors that no one can shut. Honesty will give you peace, love, life, and good relationships. It will keep your job secure if you stay sincere.

As professional nannies, we are leaders by example. You cannot give anyone something you do not have. And one of our biggest responsibilities as nannies is to be good examples in society, to live what we teach and preach about, and to let honesty be formed in us. That's what honest people do.

"Honesty is just all good."

Chapter 22

LIMITS

To be a successful nanny requires a passion turned into a career. You will need to learn to limit what you say and do. In certain situations, it requires putting *limits* on how you react and what you react to.

While being a nanny for over twenty years, I had to use a lot of wisdom in handling different situations. Growing up as kids, we spoke out too soon and without giving any thought to what we were going to say. Most of the time, we got ourselves in big trouble.

I've learned that you have to know your limits and that you can easily forsake boundaries because you grow so close to the families. Being a good nanny means you have to be careful and set limits and know where to draw the line. Remember your position; you are to be professional in every situation, as you are the employee. As you begin to build relationships with the family, you will know your limits with the family members. Don't let your guard down.

Another key to being a great nanny is staying sharp and knowing when your limits are being tested.

Linda K. Barnett

L	I	M	I	T	S
i	n	a	n	e	u
m	t	n	t	a	c
i	e	n	a	c	c
t	g	e	c	h	e
a	r	r	t		s
t	i	s			s
i	t				
o	y				
n					

(This is my interpretation of the letters in the word limits)

Chapter 23

BOUNDARIES

Nannies need to be very wise and know where to draw the line—where the boundaries are. Know how far to go and what you are allowed to (and willing to do) in every situation. That means you will need to be prepared.

When you first become a nanny, you have great zeal. You are very enthusiastic and diligently devoted to the family. This is not totally bad if you have set boundaries for yourself. You do not want to overburden yourself as well as overstep the boundaries. As a nanny, know your limits. It will help you in the long run. A nanny is a caregiver, and if you are like me, you may be a natural-born caregiver.

A nanny caregiver plays a different role than a nanny assistant. A nanny assistant is more for the parents, to assist them in whatever they need. A nanny caregiver is more for the entire family. This is why you must establish boundaries from the beginning with the family that you both have worked out together and agreed on. You have to have boundaries so you will not become bound.

You will spend a lot of time with your family in their home, on engagements and trips, as well as family affairs, so you want to be comfortable with your family. You want to enjoy being a great, happy nanny caregiver. There's nothing like enjoying your job; you see it as your work you've been called to do, as opposed to it just being a job. A red flag concerning boundaries is if you feel uncomfortable about completing a certain task, if you find yourself pondering whether you should do this or not. As you grow and come to know the family better, you will understand and know more and more about when and where to set boundaries. This will help you maintain balance so you will not become bound.

B	**O**	**U**	**N**	**D**	**A**	**R**	**Y**
o	r	**n**	e	**e**	g	**e**	o
u	d	**i**	g	**f**	r	**i**	u
n	e	**t**	o	**i**	e	**n**	t
d	r	**y**	t	**n**	e	**f**	h
a			i	**i**	m	**o**	
r			a	**t**	e	**r**	
i			t	**e**	n	**c**	
e			e		t	**e**	
s							

(This is my interpretation of the letters in the word boundary)

Chapter 24

DOCUMENTATION

It is so important that you document what happens with the children. Being a great nanny also requires you being a good reporter as well. A great nanny takes responsibility for the children's safety, always knowing whom they are with and what they are doing. It is so important that the nanny caregivers and parents work together as partners to ensure each child's needs are met. Be very observant and willing to discuss anything and everything that has been drawn to your attention.

A nanny should always have a notebook available and be ready to document at all times. This protects you and serves as a reminder to parents if they don't remember the details of a particular incident. This demonstrates you are professional, responsible, and reliable. Good documentation is a good communication tool and assists when there is lack of communication, which can lead to built-up tension. So write, write, write!

Don't just document; have the right documentation. Good documents to have accessible are documents for emergencies or trips. Children left in your care while parents are out will need permission for you to act on their behalf if medical treatment is needed. You will need documents detailing who to contact and what to do in case of an emergency. It's good to have a folder with all these documents within your reach at all times when you are on the job. You will also need to document any medications or allergies, including any foods or substances the family members are allergic to. As a nanny, you may be required to prepare some meals, so it's very important that these things are documented, especially if you're working with children with special needs. It's very important to document and report any noticeable changes immediately. The documentation is for the family's protection as well as your own.

You become a great observer. Eagerly talk to the parents about their child's daily experiences. This shows a strong commitment to the profession, and documenting demonstrates the ability to provide quality care.

The last words of wisdom I would like to share with you are vitally important to the success of a nanny's career. You must have respect, professionalism, blessing, trust, and loyalty. You will give out all these as well as receive some back while you are working with the family. For instance, you know how we go to the doctor for a check-up or if we are feeling a little sick? Sometimes we don't want anyone to know, so we trust in the doctor-patient privilege. As a nanny, it will be very important that you keep this same level of confidentiality. When you come into a family's home as their nanny, they trust you totally. Trust will be something that you earn, and it shows that you have a strong commitment to the profession.

You must respect the shared nanny-family privilege by demonstrating the ability to provide quality care.

You will become so close to the family that they will trust and confide their deepest secrets in you. So being a busybody will not keep you in this profession long. It will take wisdom, stability, love, care, loyalty, and trust to be a *great nanny.*

"He who gets wisdom loves his own soul; He who keeps understanding will find good" (Proverbs 19:8).

D	O	C	U	M	E	N	T
o	b	**o**	n	**a**	v	**e**	**r**
c	s	**m**	i	**t**	I	**w**	a
u	e	**m**	t	**e**	d	**s**	n
m	r	**u**	i	**r**	e		**s**
e	v	**n**	n	**i**	n		**m**
n	i	**i**	g	**a**	c		i
t	n	**c**		**l**	e		t
a	g	**a**					t
t		**t**					e
i		**i**					d
o		**n**					
n		**g**					

57

EPILOGUE

"Faith is taking the first step even when you can't see the whole staircase"-Martin Luther King Jr

I walked out of faith as I began to write this book trusting god as he has shown himself faithful over and over. "More than that we rejoice in our sufferings, knowing that suffering produces endurance and endurance produces character and character produces hope" Romans 5: 3-4 (NLT).

So in other words, it is good to know that I was afflicted for the GLORY of God.
The ultimate measure of a man is not where he stands in moments of comfort and convenience, but where he stands at times of challenge and controversy."

—Martin Luther King Jr.

AUTHOR BIOGRAPHY

Ms. Linda K. Barnett Ph.D (Past Having Doubt about God) is a highly respected, influential, sought after nanny encourager who shares the gospel of Jesus Christ, and speaks into the heart of all ages. She is an encouragement to many and currently resides in Tulsa, Oklahoma.

SPECIAL DEDICATIONS:

In Memory of Pinkie Bowie and the
Bowie Sisters of Okmulgee, OKIA

Charles Barnett
Curtis Bowie
Leonard Bowie

Carlin Simon
Tommy Neals Jf.

Coreen Allen
Geraldine McDade
Mattie Lyons

And most of all, my nieces:
Tiffany, Tia, ReRe, Ty, Tailynn, Trinity
and my Mother Shirley A. Neals

And all my wonderful children

CPSIA information can be obtained at www.ICGtesting.com
Printed in the USA
LVOW040749271212

313324LV00002B/162/P